C000292494

a year in the life of kingston upon thames

OLD LONDON ROAD

a year in the life of kingston upon thames

Sponsored by

gibson lane

Independent estate agents

To Ben and Jake with love.

Thanks to Nigel Botherway for proof reading the text

Pictured right: Kingston Market Place

contents

introduction

What a unique place Kingston upon Thames is. Situated in one of only four Royal boroughs in the country, it is home to both the coronation stone upon which the first king of all England was crowned and the only department store in England with a dual carriage way in the middle of it.

Sitting on the banks of the beautiful River Thames, Kingston's place in history is huge as it was the place where Royal coronations began. Edward the Elder (son of Alfred the Great) was crowned there in AD 900. Although Edward made great efforts to unite what is now England under one crown, it was his son Athelstan – crowned at Kingston in AD 925 – who finally achieved that feat and became the first man who could properly be called King of England. In all, seven Saxon kings are reputed to have been crowned in Kingston – the last of them being Ethelred the Unready, the king remembered by school children only for his funny name, crowned in AD 979.

The beating heart of the town is the ancient market square which has been ever present for definitely 800 years but probably a lot longer. Kingston was a busy inland port, a hub of trade, goods being shipped up and down the river between London and Oxford.

Kingston, being one of the few places to have a road bridge across the river, proved a good place to load and unload goods from wagon to boat and boat to wagon. Recently the market and the old quays have been given a major make over and the whole area is now thriving, full of people visiting the plethora of restaurants and bars along the river or the world food stalls in the market square. The old fruit and veg stall holders still sell their wares daily as they have for hundreds of years.

Kingston was built on trade and today the presence of John Lewis and the Bentall Centre along with a significant number of independent stores ensure it remains a busy retail centre with people coming from miles around to shop there. A weekly brick-a-brac market on the site of the old cattle market and a monthly antiques market add to it's appeal.

Kingston's transport issues have always been a talking point. Much has been written about the notorious one way system, it has in turn been described as 'the most confusing one way system in Great Britain' and 'probably the most effective of London's many gyratories and one-way systems in the cunning art of not letting you visit the town'.

When The John Lewis Partnership applied for planning permission to build their store they had to agree to build it over the road. Unfortunately for them they also encountered a prior part of the town's transport system. When digging the foundations they uncovered the remains of the 12th century ancient bridge which had to be retained for it's historical value. The area is now viewable through glass walls in the basement of the store and the area is open to the public occasionally. No other department store has roads and bridges as part of their infrastructure! The trains are another point of interest. Kingston is on a branch line whereas Surbiton has a fast train to London. Why? This was due to the past protectionism of the old coaching companies who blocked the coming of the railways to Kingston. They were latecomers to the rail revolution and hence only have a slow, plodding train service.

Kingston however has overcome all these transport issues and today is flourishing and no wonder given it's great shops, fabulous location on the river, nearby beautiful Royal parks and all only 30 minutes from central London.

The three salmon on the Kingston coat of arms represent the three fisheries mentioned in the Domesday book

Opposite: The Guildhall

winter

The River front (opposite), High Street (top) and Clattern Bridge over the Hogsmill River (bottom)

John Lewis department store straddling the dual carriageway at the beginning and end of the Kingston one way system

Kingston Bridge at night

Cold day on the river

Getting ready for business

Cafe society all year round

Early days

The earliest artefacts indicating human life around the Kingston area date back to the days when the English Channel did not exist and Britain was part of Europe. The land would have been cold and covered in snow in the winter, the remnants of the Ice Age, but in the summer the sun exposed moss and plants that would have been grazed upon by reindeer, bison and woolly rhinoceros. Where the herds grazed people followed and Stone Age axes have been found in several locations. The people who used such tools would have been nomadic Neanderthal man. Modern man appeared about 33,000 years ago and gradually replaced the Neanderthals. Another ice age ensued and the only inhabitants of Kingston were woolly mammoths whose teeth and tusks have been found locally. These ancient artefacts are found when modern buildings are being constructed and are disturbed when foundations are being dug. By the Middle Stone Age, 9,000–4,000 BC, there were people living in Ham Fields, Coombe, the Hogsmill valley as well as central Kingston. From 4,000 BC the

Neolithic or New Stone Age began. People stopped being nomadic, settled in one place and started to farm, growing crops and domesticating animals. There was definitely a settlement in Ham and almost certainly one in central Kingston. Kingston was at this time an island bounded on one side by the Thames and the other by the Hogsmill. The river would have been much wider and shallower than today and surrounded by reeds. The wildfowl and fish would have provided a ready source of food.

After the Stone Age came the Bronze Age. Bronze is a mixture of copper and tin, these two metals became highly desirable. They were found in the West Country and trade routes were bringing the valuable elements to metal producing centres for the production of bronze. One important trade route was the Thames and Kingston was one of the metal producing centres to be found on the river. Beautiful bronze weapons found in the Thames near Kingston testify to the prosperity of the area.

Archaeological finds from the late Bronze Age

and early Iron Age from the area are in short supply indicating that settlements may have moved to higher ground such as Caesar's Camp – an Iron Age fort to be found on Royal Wimbledon golf course. Kingston was obviously not a very important place in the Iron Age, or come to that in the time of the Roman invasion of England.

The Romans had first attempted to invade Britain when Julius Caesar invaded in 55 BC. That foray was a failure but they returned in 43 AD and remained here until 410 AD. They only left in order to defend Rome from the invading Northern German tribes. They changed Britain forever leaving us with a new language, a calendar that endures today with the months of the year named after Roman gods and rulers, straight roads and under floor heating amongst other things. The area around Kingston was definitely settled and cultivated by Romans, but as yet no town existed.

Rowing in the fog

The towpath on a frosty morning

Beautiful frosty morning in Bushy Park

Richmond Park

Richmond Park is the largest and most well known of the three parks that surround the town. In 1637 Charles I built a wall around 2,500 acres of private and common land that stretched from Kingston to Roehampton and Richmond. The land was acquired legally and illegally, with and without the permission of landowners. In doing so, even though he already had a substantial deer park in Home Park, just down the road between Kingston and Hampton Court, and one in Old Deer Park, in Richmond, he created another even larger deer park for himself whilst taking no regard of local opinion. Needless to say this caused outrage locally and was largely due to his repetitive arrogant behavior, such as this, that later cost the King his head. Now, however, 400 years later, we reap the unforeseen benefits of his actions with the beautiful park untouched by the ever present development of land outside its walls.

As well as being much larger than Home Park and Bushy Park, Richmond Park is wilder and hilly. It is full of ancient oak trees that are largely responsible for its value as a wildlife area. It is of national and international importance for wildlife conservation, being a Site of Special Scientific Interest (SSSI), a National Nature Reserve (NNR) and Special Area of Conservation (SAC).

The largest Site of Special Scientific Interest in London, it was designated as an SSSI in 1992. It has a range of habitats of value to wildlife. In particular, it is of importance for its diverse deadwood beetle fauna associated with the ancient trees found throughout the parkland, particularly the stag beetle. In addition, the park supports the most extensive area of dry acid grassland in Greater London. The park was designated as an SAC in 2005, signifying the park is now considered to be of international significance. A single mature oak tree is known to be able to support an amazing 284 different types of insect. The horse chestnut only supports approximately five different types. It is truly an enormously bio diverse eco system in its own right. Many of the trees in the park are 600 years old.

The park still has a herd of 650 fallow and red deer roaming freely. No longer hunted, they are managed by the park's gamekeepers, who conduct an annual cull. In the summer they give birth in the long grass where the young are hidden by their mothers until strong enough to follow the herd. It is possible to stumble upon these cute bambi like creatures whilst walking, but resist the temptation to handle them. They have not been abandoned and there will almost certainly be a rather protective mother nearby who will happily attack a dog, or human, in defence of its young. This is a time of year to give due respect to these semi-wild animals. The other time of year when they are to be given a wide berth is during the rutting season in the autumn. The mating season is when the males strut around bellowing and fighting with other males for the right to control a harem of does. All the animals are on edge at this time and although it is amazing to watch their antics, it is best done at a safe distance.

Within the park is the beautiful Isabella Plantation, a woodland garden which is home to a wonderful collection of azaleas which are at their best in May. However, the garden is a lovely place to stroll at any time of year and there are always interesting trees and plants to see as well as the wildlife on the ponds, one of which is home to a collection of wildfowl, along with carp weighing more than 30lb.

There are plenty of places to eat and drink, most car parks have vans selling drinks and delicious bacon sandwiches which go down well after a walk or cycle ride, but the jewel in the crown is Pembroke Lodge. Fantastically situated with views over the Thames Valley below, the lodge has been tastefully renovated after it fell into a state of disrepair. It was once home to a former Prime Minister, Sir John Russell, and his famous philosopher grandson Bertrand Russell.

Today there is a cafe outside for dog owners and another inside in a dog-free zone with more substantial choices, where on a nice day you can sit on the terrace and admire the view. There are lovely gardens around the lodge and from one area, known as Henry VIII's Mound, it is possible to glimpse St. Paul's Cathedral through a tree lined vista.

Kingston is truly blessed to be surrounded by these three Royal beautiful parks.

Opposite: Snowy antlers
Left: Mist over Pen Ponds

Eden Walk Shopping Centre (top); famous independent record store, Banquet Records (bottom)

The tunnel to the Bentall Centre from the car parks (right)

Football old and new

In 1790 some Kingston residents were in court after being accused of 'riot'. This riotous behaviour referred to, occurred at the 'Shrove Tuesday football match' held annually in the town. The accused claimed that they were recreating a game played since early medieval times which commemorated a victory in battle over the invading Danes. After this battle the Danish leader supposedly had his head chopped off and it was subsequently used as a football. This story was widespread all over the country and games of 'shrove Tuesday football' were played every year from north to south and east to west from early medieval times until relatively recently.

The game started at 11 o'clock on the morning of Shrove Tuesday when hundreds of men congregated in the market place near 'The Druids Head' public house and finished at 5pm. There were two teams, one representing the Thames Street half of the town and the other representing the Town's end.

The ball was kicked about all over the town for 6 hours and whoever kicked it over the path across the market place at 5pm was considered the winner. Everyone would then retire to the pub for a jolly good celebration. Mostly it was good hearted fun but it was also a time when old scores were settled and over the years it became more rowdy with increased drunkenness and fighting. The townspeople began to get fed up with the damage caused and the unruly behaviour of some of the participants. It was eventually stopped in 1867.

By this time a slightly more organised version of football was being played regularly not restricted to the once yearly free for all that was the Shrove Tuesday football match. Public schools used to play but they each had their own rules. So it would be possible to play matches against each other a set of universally agreed rules had to be written and adopted by all participants. In 1863 the Football Association was formed and the first set of the rules of football were published. Two years later Kingston got its own officially recognised football team. Kingstonian was formed in autumn 1885, under the name Kingston & Surbiton YMCA.

Today Kingstonian are a semi-professional team playing in the Isthmian League, which is a league featuring semi-professional and amateur clubs from London, East and South East England. They share their ground, the Kingsmeadow Stadium with AFC Wimbledon who took over the lease of the site in 2003 when the old Wimbledon FC split in two.

In March 2017, but for an extremely large police presence there would have been another football related riot in Kingston. It was the historic evening when MK Dons came to play AFC Wimbledon for the first time in the football league. In the programme the MK Dons were merely referred to as 'Milton Keynes'. There is such acrimony between these clubs that trouble was forecast but the match passed off peacefully with the home side winning 2-0 and going above their arch rivals in the league. Why the hatred?

In August 2001, Wimbledon FC announced its intent to relocate to Milton Keynes. Despite opposition from the majority of Wimbledon fans, The Football League and The Football Association gave the club permission to do so. They completed the move and were renamed the MK (Milton Keynes) Dons. Their formerly loyal but now outraged fans deserted that team and went on to form a new club, AFC Wimbledon, which came to play in Kingston.

AFC Wimbledon is now fully professional, playing in League Two of the Football League, the same league as MK Dons. When AFC Wimbledon was formed, it started at the bottom and was semi professional. In its short history, the club has been extremely successful, being promoted five times in nine seasons, and going up from the ninth tier (Combined Counties Premier) to the fourth (League Two). AFC Wimbledon hold the record of the longest unbeaten run of league matches in English senior football, having played 78 consecutive league games without a defeat.

Kingsmeadow has recently been sold to Chelsea FC so what will happen in the future is as yet uncertain.

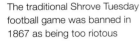

The traditional Shrove Tuesday football game was banned in 1867 as being too riotous

Adoring AFC Wimbledon fans

Mosaics around the town

Surbiton

Surbiton was put on the map by the 1970s TV sitcom, 'The Good Life'. Tom and Barbara Good, a couple who decide to drop out from society and become self sufficient, live next door to the conservative, conformist, social-climbing couple, Jerry and Margo Leadbetter in The Avenue, Surbiton, Surrey. It was a hugely popular programme, taking a gentle poke at life in the suburbs and the craze for self sufficiency which was prevalent at the time.

There does seem to be something about Surbiton that comedians find amusing. In the 1990s, 'Stella Street', was a comedy/documentary spoof in which celebrities find refuge in Surbiton from the madness of their famous lives in the banality of suburbia. And last but not least in the early 1970s the Monty Python team did a sketch about Mr and Mrs Brian Norris who set out to prove that the inhabitants of Hounslow could have been descendants of the people of Surbiton who had made the great trek north. Although these programmes were all set in Surbiton, none of them were actually filmed there, a variety of locations elsewhere in London being used instead.

So how did Surbiton become such an archetypical suburb worthy of mockery? Probably because its name so resembles the word suburb. After Stella Street it was sometimes nicknamed 'Suburbiton'. There is evidence that a settlement has existed on the site since at least 1179. At the time, it was known as Suberton, meaning sub-South, Bereton-Granary in Saxon. It was separated from Norbiton or the north granary by the Hogsmill River. Before the arrival of the railway, Surbiton was little more than a farm. Maps from as late as the early 19th century show it as little more than a crossroads, but that all changed with the coming of the railways.

The town started to prosper when a plan to build the main railway line down to the south coast closer to nearby Kingston was rejected by Kingston council, fearing the detrimental effect it would have on the busy coaching trade. This resulted in the line being routed further south, through a cutting in the hill south of Surbiton. Surbiton railway station opened in 1838, and was originally named Kingston-upon-Railway, and was only renamed Surbiton to distinguish it from the new Kingston station on the Shepperton branch line which did not open until 1 January 1869. As a result of Kingston council's decision, Surbiton now has a fast train to London which takes only 18 minutes to reach Waterloo, whereas Kingston is still only on a branch line making Surbiton much more desirable to commuters. In 1936 a new Art Deco station was built, replacing the old original station. Today this is a Grade II listed building.

An illiterate but entrepreneurial brewer called Thomas Pooley is given credit for initially developing the area around the station. He saw the possibilities that new transport links brought, purchased 100 acres of farm land and built many splendid houses on the land around the station. Like many an aspiring property developer since, however, Pooley went bankrupt in the process, so he never saw the fruits of his foresight. There is some evidence that the authorities in Kingston who wanted to protect their coaching businesses were annoyed by his success and made life difficult for this upstart and contributed to his demise.

Today Surbiton is flourishing with a population of nearly 40,000 people.

Opposite left: An example of a Thomas Pooley house

Opposite right: Surbiton clock tower built to commemorate the coronation of Edward VII

Below: Grade II-listed Art Deco Surbiton railway station

The late Victorian Assembly Rooms now part of Surbiton Girls' School

The Edwardian Surbiton Coronation Hall

Kingston Library (bottom) and old Empire Music Hall Theatre (top)

The market open for custom come rain or shine

Ham, Hampton Court and Chessington

The town of Kingston is very lucky to be surrounded on all sides by famous and wonderful tourist attractions.

To the North is Ham House, situated in the pretty urban village of Ham, it was originally built in 1610. William Murray was gifted it in 1626 by his close friend Charles I who was a regular visitor. William, like the king, was a man of style with a taste for the latest fashions in architecture, art and interior design. He refurbished the original house in a lavish way and Ham House became an entertainment hub in the court of Charles I until he unfortunately lost his head following the bloody English Civil War. William's daughter Elizabeth, in charge of the house during the 'Commonwealth of England' years, managed somehow to have good relations with the Lord Protector Oliver Cromwell and remain in touch with the exiled Stuart prince. Obviously a canny operator. When Charles II was restored to power in 1660, Ham House again became a Royal 'hang out', a place of extravagance and entertaining. It was considered one of the grandest houses of the Stuart era. Today it is owned by the National Trust and remains a fine example of indulgent 17th century living.

To the west a few miles up stream from Kingston on the banks of the River Thames is Hampton Court Palace. It was built by Cardinal Wolsey in 1514, on the site of a manor once owned by the crusaders, the Knights Hospitallers of St. John of Jerusalem (now known as St. John's Ambulance), and was his pride and joy being such a magnificent place. Wolsey was a close friend and confidant to Henry VIII, he was his Cardinal and his Lord Chancellor and was often referred to as' alter rex' or 'other king' because of the power he held. However, Cardinal Wolsey's failure to secure an annulment for Henry's marriage to Catherine of Aragon led to a falling out between the two and a loss of his power. Wolsey saw the writing on the wall and before the king could take the palace, the Cardinal gave it to him as a gift.

Henry expanded the palace and his additions included amongst other things new kitchens to feed his vast entourage, a tennis court and a communal toilet which could take 30 people at each sitting and became known as 'the great house of easement'. All of the Tudor and Stuart kings and queens regularly stayed there with the Georgian king, George II, being the last Royal resident. Queen Victoria opened it to the public in 1838 and it has been a popular tourist attraction ever since. Annually in July it hosts the largest flower show in the world.

To the south of Kingston town at the bottom tip of the borough is Chessington World of Adventures. Originally a zoo, the theme park aspect was added in 1987 when the number of visitors to the zoo started to decline. Since then it has grown in popularity and is now along with Alton Towers and Thorpe Park one of the country's most popular theme parks. The mansion in the park known today as the Burnt Stub was originally built in 1348. In the English Civil War it became a Royalist stronghold, and Oliver Cromwell's Parliamentary forces burnt it to the ground hence it's name. Today Burnt Stub houses the attraction Hocus Pocus Hall.

To the east of the town is Richmond Park whose importance to the area means it warrants its own section in this book.

All these attractions add to the appeal of the town itself and make Kingston a very desirable place to visit and live.

Left: Chessington World of Adventures

Right: Hampton Court Palace

Opposite: Ham House and Old Father Thames (top) and The Royal Ballet School, Richmond Park (bottom)

Murals and mosaics in Ham

spring

Enjoying the spring sunshine

From village to town

One of the most memorable dates in English history, 1066, saw the defeat of King Harold, the last Saxon king, by William the Conqueror, the first of the Norman kings. William wanted to know all about his new kingdom, and how much he could tax his people, so he commissioned a survey.

Men were sent all over the country to assess the extent of the land and resources owned in England at the time. The information collected was recorded by hand in two huge books, in the space of around a year. William died before it was fully completed. It was written by an observer of the survey that: "There was no single hide nor a yard of land, nor indeed one ox nor one cow nor one pig which was left out".

The grand and comprehensive scale of the Domesday survey, and the irreversible nature of the information collated, led people to compare it to the Last Judgement, or Doomsday, described in the Bible, when the deeds of Christians written in the Book of Life were to be placed before God for judgement. This name was not adopted until the late 12th century.

Kingston was described in the Domesday book as a 'vill', inhabited by 'villeins' with land for 32 ploughs,

40 acres of meadow, woodland, five mills and three fisheries. The survey was taken in 1085 and published a year later. It is thought that about 500 people lived there – quite a large population at the time, sustained by working on the land, fishing and milling. Over the next hundred years Kingston prospered and came to be recognised as one of the main settlements in Surrey.

The Kingston Carta (charter) signed in 1200 by King John was not as important to history as the Magna Carta, signed 15 years later, but was significant to the people who lived and worked in the town, and for its future growth.

It helped change Kingston's status from a village to a town. A charter was granted when the king accepted that Kingston was a place capable of managing its own affairs, with leaders to represent it and people living there working in different trades, industries and occupations. All this was a great departure from the village of 100 years before.

Over that century, a new grand stone church, All Saints, had been built on the site of the old Minster, bringing crafts people to the area. And the ford that

crossed the Thames from Hampton Wick to the gravel island known as Kingston had been replaced by a wooden bridge with stone footings that can still be seen today beneath the John Lewis department store. The bridge at Kingston was the first one upstream after London Bridge and was of strategic importance to a king trying to keep his barons under control. A stone bridge over the Hogsmill River, Clattern Bridge, had also been built, linking Kingston to Guildford. The Hogsmill river was named after John Hogg, owner of a mill on that River and it is thought the bridge got its name because of the clattering noise horses hooves made when crossing it.

In the space of 100 years from when the Domesday book was written to when its first charter was granted, Kingston had transformed itself from a village concerned with farming and fishing to a town, thriving with its market, industries, and traders.

Mock Tudor building in the market place adorned with images depicting the history of the town, built for Boots the Chemist in 1909

All Saints Church (opposite) and the Coronation Stone (below)

Previous spread: Pretty in pink; All Saints Church
Fun amongst the magnolia, All Saints churchyard

Flying high at the Skate Park in Hampton Wick with
the trophy shoes hanging proudly in the branches

Left: Spring blossom, Kings Passage   Right: Kings Road

Opposite: Canbury Gardens

Bushy Park

At 1,100 acres, Bushy Park is the second largest of London's Royal Parks. Like Home Park, it stretches from the Hampton Wick side of Kingston Bridge as far as Hampton Court in the west and Teddington in the north. Originally medieval farmland, with visible remnants of the feudal field systems still present, it became a deer park during the reign of Henry VIII. One of Henry's first acts was to chop down many mature oak trees to build ships for his navy. He then planted many replacement saplings and surrounded them with prickly hawthorn bushes to protect them from being nibbled by the deer. It is believed that these bushes gave the park its name.

Within the park are three grand houses. Hampton Court House was built by the second Earl of Halifax, who gave his name to Halifax in Nova Scotia. He built the house for his mistress, who he employed as his governess whilst he shipped her husband off to a lucrative job in the West Indies.

The next encumbrance was an equally colourful character, the fourth Earl of Sandwich – yes, he who gave his name to the sandwich. Supposedly, whilst pursuing his obsession with gambling, he didn't like to leave the tables to take time out to eat, so ordered his servants to bring him two slices of bread with meat inside that he could munch at his leisure. His friends started to refer to this as a 'sandwich'. He also used Hampton Court House for his mistress to live in. She was Martha Rey, an infamous singer, who bore him five children and was eventually murdered by another jealous lover. Today the beautiful house is a school and expensive wedding venue.

Bushy House was thought to have started life as a stand for the public to watch rabbit coursing, the forerunner to greyhound racing, which was a popular gambling pursuit with the masses in Tudor times. The most interesting resident was William, Duke of Clarence, the third son of William III. Never expected to be king, he was a bit of a waster. He lived in the park with his mistress, the actress Dora Jordan, whose earnings helped keep him. She bore him 10 children and they lived happily together for 20 years until her earning powers started to fade and it became apparent that William was going to become king. She was summarily packed off to France where she died a pauper. Her children by the king were given the name FitzClarence and David Cameron, the former British Prime Minister, is one of her descendants.

William then married a rich wife, Princess Adelaide of Saxe Meiningen. She had no children that survived long, so William had no heirs, allowing his niece, Victoria, to become queen on his death. She was not interested in the house, however, and gave it to the National Physical Laboratory, who still use it today.

Upper Lodge is the oldest occupied site in the park, probably starting life as a Roman marching fort. Various keepers of the park lived there and in 1709 the 1st Earl of Halifax took over the house and re-built it, along with a beautiful water garden. This garden was neglected over the years until it was a complete wilderness.

The historian Roy Strong, whilst doing an inventory of paintings in the Royal Collection, stumbled upon a picture called 'Figures in a Garden' depicting people strolling in the water gardens. The Friends of Bushy

Park took on the challenge of recreating the old gardens and they were opened to the public in 2009, 300 years after they were originally opened.

The house itself went on to have various uses. It was a convalescent home for Canadian soldiers during the First World War and after the war it became a holiday school for poor boys from the East End who were suffering from respiratory diseases. During the Second World War it housed the supreme headquarters of the Allied Expeditionary Force headed by General Eisenhower, who planned the D-Day landings there.

The park is home to 90 red deer and 140 fallow deer, all of whom wander freely, grazing on the acid grassland which, along with the ancient trees, led to the park being designated a Site of Special Scientific Interest and so is protected. In the middle of the park are a series of lovely ponds, the Diana, Heron and Leg of Mutton, all fed by the Longford River and built by Oliver Cromwell so he could fish there. Today, the biggest carp weigh over 40lbs.

Chestnut Avenue dissects the park with its mile-long straight avenue of chestnut trees with the Diana fountain as its centrepiece. When William and Mary came to the throne they wanted to revamp Hampton Court Palace. Sir Christopher Wren designed the avenue to be the approach to the new entrance that was planned, but Queen Mary died unexpectedly of smallpox so the renovations never happened and the grand avenue now leads to nowhere in particular.

There are two linked, recently restored woodland gardens in the west of the park which are full of beautiful azaleas, daffodils, cherry trees and fine examples of the peculiar swamp Cyprus tree with its weird overground root system. In one wood there is a hugely popular cafe called The Pheasantry, after the area's original use. In Henry VIII's time pheasants for hunting and the table were bred there.

The entrance to Bushy Park from Kingston takes you along a short path with King's Field Skate Park on the left and allotments on the right. Look up into the trees by the skate park and you will see hundreds of pairs of trainers. Apparently they are shoes that have been worn whilst practicing a particularly difficult trick and when it has been mastered the shoes get thrown up the tree to celebrate.

The Diana fountain in Bushy Park

Daffodils in Bushy Park, azaleas in Richmond Park, catkins in the Ham Lands, box and lavender in Ham House gardens

Crocuses in Canbury Gardens near the Boaters Inn

Retail

Kingston has had a very long relationship with shops and shopping. Borough deeds mention the presence of shops around the market place in 1315 and from then until the 19th century, small specialist shops ruled the roost on the High Street. Frank Bentall, referred to as "the man who made Kingston", changed all that.

In 1867, at the age of 24, he bought a struggling drapers shop in Clarence Street and set about growing a profitable business, aiming to impress his future father-in-law. He proved to be extremely successful. His profit grew from £70 to £200 within a year, and he used the money to buy neighbouring shops. His son Leonard continued in his father's footsteps and, by 1947, Bentalls had expanded to become the largest privately owned store in Europe.

Bentalls was refurbished in the 1930s, with the new facade modelled on Sir Christopher Wren's architectural style at nearby Hampton Court Palace. When the old building was knocked down and refurbished in the late 1980s, this facade was retained.

At the same time as the Bentall Centre was being re-developed, a brand new John Lewis store was being built on the site of the old horse fair across the road. Formerly on the edge of town the area was used for an annual horse fair. When the fairs stopped, houses started to be built there but in the 1930s the householders were evicted and the land was cleared

for re-development.

The Second World War intervened, however, and the area remained derelict and was used as a car park until John Lewis came along. The department store straddles the road still named 'Horsefair'.

The 1980s and 90s was a time of great investment and change in Kingston, with the Eden Walk shopping centre undergoing a major makeover at the same time as the other new stores were being built. The original shopping centre was conceived in 1936 when Kingston Council was one of the first local authorities in Britain to recognise the need for a multi-storey car park. Amazingly it took 34 years to actually be built, eventually opening in 1967. It could easily have been called Heathen Walk shopping centre were it not for a man called John Dawson.

Dawson was an influential and religious man who was embarrassed to both live and worship on Heathen Street so used his considerable influence to

change its name to his preferred Eden Street. Marks and Spencer was one of the original shops in the new shopping centre and when it was re-furbished in 1995 the company took the opportunity to enlarge its Kingston store and it became one of the flagship M&S stores in the UK.

At the turn of the 20th century, when Frank Bentall was expanding his empire, another entrepreneur, Sir Jesse Boot, decided to open another of his chemist shops in Kingston. He liked his shops to have an antique look, so when he took over a shop in the Market Place he gave the shop a mock Tudor frontage with the history of Kingston depicted on it. Today many people believe it is truly a Tudor building, when in fact, it is the little shop next door on the corner that is the authentic one.

Today Kingston is a thriving retail centre, a magnet for shoppers from all over south east of England, a great alternative for those who don't fancy going all the way into London.

The two big department stores in Kingston with the Bentall Centre trying to replicate the architecture of Hampton Court Palace

'Out of order' sculpture by David Mach

1960s buildings   Above: Tolworth Tower

Shop displays around town

Monday market on the site of the Old Cattle Market

The River

Thousands of years ago, central Kingston was an island of gravel in the middle of a much wider and shallower River Thames. The river has shaped the town's development; from the time when the first Stone Age men fished there until today, where it provides the backdrop to a modern cafe society.

Artefacts found by archaeologists indicate that nomadic Stone Age man made use of the river's many resources, and from 1500 BC, in the Bronze Age, the Thames was a major artery for the distribution of copper and tin when Kingston flourished as a metal-producing centre. The area dwindled in importance during the Iron Age, however, as the demand for copper and tin diminished with the rise in the use of iron.

There had always been a ford at Kingston making it one of the few places along the Thames where it was possible to cross the river. This was of huge significance and one of the reasons that it grew as a site of importance. The Victorian historian W D Biden was convinced "beyond all doubt" that the ford Caesar's army used to cross the Thames when he invaded in 54 BC was the one at Kingston. There is little evidence to support Biden, but it is indisputable that the river provided ease of access for trade and travel. The ability to transfer goods from road to river and vice versa was pivotal in Kingston's growth.

By the end of the 12th century, Kingston was considered to be a town, with its central island surrounded by mud and marsh and two bridges providing access. A wooden bridge over the main river joined Kingston to Hampton Wick, and Clattern Bridge crossed the Hogsmill inlet. The main bridge over the Thames was built for the sole purpose of maintaining political and military control being the only river crossing for miles and therefore of strategic importance.

As a by-product, land trade prospered, but river trade suffered because the struts supporting the bridge made it difficult for boats to navigate through it. Repairs were also costly. The cost of mending damage caused by floods and other events were crippling the town financially by the early 14th century. To alleviate the situation Edward II granted the town the right to charge to cross the bridge. These tolls helped pay for future repairs. Ships passing under it were also, rather unfairly, obliged to pay a toll.

The fees were hugely unpopular until the bridge became toll free in 1565, thanks to a rich benefactor named Robert Hammond, who, on his death, bequeathed money annually to go towards bridge repairs, thus negating the need for tolls.

By the 16th century Kingston was considered a thriving inland port with timber, pottery and fish being shipped to London and stone and wine offloaded in Kingston and distributed by road to the rest of southern England. There were busy wharfs on both sides of the Hogsmill with mills, breweries, timber and coal yards nearby. Transport was still easier, safer and cheaper by boat than road and courtiers could pay watermen to row them to Hampton Court or Richmond palaces.

Fishing was still an important industry and the fishermen came into conflict with the watermen because their fish traps and weirs obstructed the passage of the watermen's barges. It had also become a centre for boat building. One of the boat builders, established in 1777, was Turks, who still operate passenger boats today.

The bridge at Kingston remained the first one upstream after London Bridge until 1729 when a bridge was built at Putney. The old dilapidated wooden bridge that always was in need of repair was finally replaced with an elegant new stone bridge in 1828. With the new bridge came the return of the hated tolls as money was needed to pay for the cost of building it. When it became toll free again in 1870 there was a massive celebration in the town.

Throughout the history of the bridge the sheer weight of numbers crossing it had constantly brought the need for repairs. This was no different in medieval or modern times. In the 1990s the bridge was once again collapsing under the weight of the traffic. Work started to repair and widen it in 1998 and three years later it was completed with the new bridge being twice as wide as the old one. All this was done without the bridge ever closing – and no toll was levied this time!

As the years have gone by, river usage has switched from commercial to recreational. Kingston Rowing Club has produced many international oarsmen and women over the years, and annual regattas have been held for the past 150 years. In more recent times, dragon boat racing has also become a popular attraction. Turks launches still transport people up and down on their pleasure steamers. Charter Quay was redeveloped at the millennium and has provided the town with a great selection of cafes and restaurants which are buzzing on a summer's evening.

The River Thames was flowing through the English countryside for years before people decided to settle by its banks and no doubt it will continue to flow after we have gone, but there is no doubting its influence and how it shaped Kingston's history.

Opposite: St.Raphael's Catholic Church peeping out through the hawthorn blossom on the river

Below: Painting al fresco outside the Boaters Inn

Boathouses along the river

Kingston Bridge and Charter Quay

summer

The view from Kingston Bridge

That Famous Place

Towards the end of their 400 year stay in Britain, the Romans were increasingly beleaguered. Picts from Scotland, Scots from Ireland and Saxons from Germany all saw the great Roman Empire beginning to weaken and attempted to take advantage.

When the last Roman legions finally cut their losses and left in 410 AD, the void was filled by the Angles, Saxons and Jutes from northern Germany and Denmark. They had been working for the Romans as mercenaries for hundreds of years and when their employers left they took over the mantle of rulers of England. These people were illiterate, without the sophistication of the Romans, and little is known of the first few hundred years of their occupation. This is the period of history when legends like that of King Arthur flourished. The dark ages had begun.

To begin with, the Anglo-Saxon rule was fragmented, the country divided into seven kingdoms, Northumbria, Mercia, Wessex, East Anglia, Essex, Kent and Sussex. Kingston lay on the border of the two strongest kingdoms, Wessex and Mercia. Possibly because of it's geographical significance, the town's importance increased as the Saxon rule progressed.

The name Kingston is of Saxon origin, Cyninges (kings) tun (estate). It is believed that a significant Saxon church or minster was present, probably on the site of All Saints Church in the centre of today's town. The Saxon chronicle tells of a meeting between King Egbert and the Archbishop of Canterbury at Cyninges, "that famous place in Surrey," in 838.

The council proved to be far reaching and meaningful, creating a pact of mutual co-operation between church and state that still exists today. In 925 the first King of England was crowned in Kingston. King Athelstan, a mighty warrior, was the first Saxon king to rule over all the Saxon kingdoms and therefore first to unite the whole of England into a single kingdom. He was also the first king to be 'crowned'. Previous kings wore helmets; Athelstan was the first to wear a crown.

There is solid evidence that Athelstan and Ethelred the Unready were crowned in Kingston, and the five other Saxon kings were almost certainly crowned there as well, even though the evidence supporting that belief is much sketchier. The stone thought likely to be the coronation stone sits proudly outside the Guildhall, but there are plans to relocate it to All Saints Church, nearer to the site of the coronations.

For many years the stone was overlooked, used as a mounting block in the market place, and wasn't considered historically significant until 1850. Whether or not it really is the coronation stone will never be truly known, yet its presence is a constant reminder to the inhabitants of the town that their Kingston was the place where the first king of England was crowned and that is something to be proud of.

Despite the advances of the Vikings in the north and the east, the Saxons continued to rule England until the Normans arrived in 1066 and Kingston continued to thrive.

Opposite: The coronation stone near the Guildhall

Below: 14c painting of St.Blaise on a pillar in All Saints Church

Mural of the kings crowned in Kingston in Eden Street

Surrey County Hall

Kingston Crown Court

Ham House and Ham Lands

Seething Wells

Up until the mid 19th century, Seething Wells was notable only for the presence of hot springs where people would bathe their eyes thinking that the water had healing properties and for being a place where gentlemen would house their mistresses.

That all changed when in 1848 the Lambeth Water Company decided to move their supply and extract and filter water from further upstream of London. The Thames water at Seething Wells was considered 'pure, constant and abundant' by the chief engineer James Simpson and he recommended that it would be the best place to re-locate their business.

Work began in 1849 with 800 navvies employed on the site. It was a huge undertaking with extremely deep filter beds being first dug then layers of sand, gravel and shells added. Water was pumped into the beds from the river. It was cleansed as gravity worked it through the filtration layers. The clean water was collected into ceramic pipes deep in the ground and fed into one 10 mile long cast iron pipe that stretched all the way to London. The first clean water arrived in London in 1852.

After the success of the filter beds at Seething Wells the Chelsea Water Company also re-located

to the area and built vast filter beds all along the river to Ravens Ait. These two companies in competition with each other continued to expand and to supply the ever increasing population of London with water extracted from the Thames at Kingston.

The Thames in London in the 19th century was an open sewer and in the middle of the century things came to a head with the summer named the 'Great Stink'. That particular summer, all of London was feeling the affects of an oppressive heat wave and as a result, all the sewage in the Thames began to ferment in the scorching sun – centuries of waste was literally cooking in the monstrous heat. The result was a smell as offensive and disgusting as can ever be imagined. It spawned accounts such as the following: there were "stories flying of men struck down with the stench, and of all kinds of fatal diseases, up-springing on the river's banks". The most common 'fatal' disease of the time was cholera. All through the 19th century cholera had decimated communities in London. A particularly devastating outbreak in Soho in 1854 was the stimulus to a Covent Garden GP named John Snow to find the cause of this disease. At the time it was commonly thought that it was an

airborne disease but Dr Snow was convinced it came from a polluted water source, he just had to prove it. He tracked deaths in the Soho area and found that all of the people who were dying were drinking from the same communal water pump. He produced a 'ghost map' showing the deaths and their location relative to the position of the pump he thought was the culprit. He later researched the death rate from cholera of people in the Lambeth area who were all drinking the clean water from Seething Wells. He proved that people that drank clean water did not fall ill from cholera. He is considered one of the fathers of modern epidemiology. His findings inspired fundamental changes in the water and waste systems of London, which led to similar changes in other cities, and a significant improvement in general public health around the world.

Many of the filtration beds and tunnels still exist providing a rich habitat for wildlife and are today a conservation area. Some of the Victorian buildings have been incorporated into the Seething Wells campus part of Kingston University.

Kingston University Seething Wells Campus

Opposite: Seething Wells reservoirs

Kingston Rowing Regatta

The Dragon Boat Racing Regatta

Aviation

At first glance it was a strange decision for Thomas Sopwith to base his aviation business in Kingston, a rural market town known as a centre for retail, as opposed to a industrial manufacturing. On reflection, however, there was method in his madness. He was a relatively local lad, born in Kensington, who learned to fly and formed an aviation school at Brooklands Airfield in nearby Weybridge in 1910. He knew craftsmen had been employed in boat building in the town for centuries and that their skills would be transferable to building aircraft instead.

Sopwith was a fascinating and extraordinary man. He was the eighth child and only son of Thomas Sopwith senior, an engineer. At the age of 10 on a family holiday in Scotland a loaded gun that he was holding accidentally went off killing his father, an incident that haunted him his whole life. He learned to fly aged 22, set up his first aircraft factory aged 24 and by 30 his fighters dominated the skies over the Western Front. He always had an obsession with machines, originally motorbikes and at the age of 16 took part in a 100 mile tri-car race where he ended up a medal winner. He was also an excellent ice skater, playing ice hockey for Great Britain and winning a gold medal at the first ever European championships in 1910. Ironically the first Sopwith factory in Kingston was on the site of the old Edwardian skating rink in the town.

He set up his first company with Fred Sigrist, an engineer and designer, and a flamboyant Australian test pilot named Harry Hawker. These three pioneers designed the legendary Camel, the best all-round fighter plane in the First World War. The pilot who shot down the legendary Red Baron was flying a Sopwith Camel.

The aircraft they built were revolutionary, but also practical. Thanks to their cunning designs and an efficient manufacturing operation, Sopwith achieved market saturation in WWI, but after the war liquidated the company, possibly to avoid punitive post-war taxes. The three re-entered the aviation business a few years later with a new firm named after his chief engineer and test pilot, Harry Hawker. Sopwith became chairman of the new firm, Hawker Aircraft.

Hawker was killed on 12 July 1921 when the plane he was flying crashed over Hendon. After a post mortem he was found to have been suffering from spinal tuberculosis which may have contributed to his fatal crash. He was only 32. The king sent a message of condolence, asserting that: "The nation had lost one of its most distinguished airmen". Hawker is buried in St Paul's Church, Hook, Chessington, Surrey.

Hawker Siddeley Aircraft was formed in 1935 as a result of the purchase by Hawker Aircraft of the companies of JD Siddeley. During the Second World War, Hawker Siddeley was one of the United Kingdom's most important aviation concerns, producing numerous designs including the famous Hawker Hurricane fighter that, along with the Spitfire, formed Britain's front-line defence in the Battle of Britain. During this campaign, Hurricanes outnumbered all other British fighters, combined, in service and were responsible for shooting down 55 per cent of all enemy aircraft.

By 1977, when it was nationalised into British Aerospace, Sir Thomas Sopwith's Hawker Siddeley Aviation owned half of Britain's aircraft industry. The Kingston team went on to develop and produce advanced versions of the Harrier and Hawk with McDonnell Douglas in America. The aviation industry was the largest employer in Kingston for most of the 20th century. 27,000 Kingston designed aircraft were built between 1920 and 1992. Kingston designed aircraft have served continuously with the British Air Force since 1914.

BAe closed the last site in the 1990s. Sopwith himself lived to the ripe old age of 101, with his 100th birthday marked by a fly-past of military aircraft over his home. His legacy to the town is huge. He established three factories in Kingston, meaning a small town in the commuter belt was responsible for the majority of fighter designs in WWI and WWII and was at the heart of Britain's military aviation industry for years afterwards. He became one of Kingston's largest employers with entire households dependent on Sopwith's pay packets. The town has a lot to thank him for. What's left today to remind us of this legacy? Some streets bearing relevant names, a housing estate, the YMCA Hawker Centre and Kingston University runs undergraduate courses in aviation and has a building and a scholarship named after Sopwith's top designer, Sir Sydney Camm.

The weekly 5k Parkrun starts and finishes at the Hawker Centre

The propellors built into the railings in Canbury Park Road commemorating the importance of the aviation business to the area

Ride London

Historic market town

It is fitting that Historic Market Town signs greet visitors as they enter Kingston, as there has been a market in the town, situated near All Saints Church, since the 12th century. It was originally held on a Sunday but the church began to object that worshippers were being distracted from their prayers, so market days were changed to Wednesday and Saturday.

The market was then, as it is now, at the heart of the town. Trade was central to Kingston's growth and the market was central to its trade. A new bridge built around 1170 opened up valuable transport links, supplementing and complementing the already busy river trade. Goods were brought by road to the thriving inland port and transferred to boats for the onward journey and vice versa.

The bridge was the first one above London, making Kingston the first crossing point over the Thames after the city. Records of tolls on goods passing over the new bridge, presumably on their way to market, includes wine, hogs, timber, butter, salmon, salt, arrows, nails and cloth.

Henry III granted the men of Kingston the right to have a guild merchant. This was a society of tradesmen and this particular guild had four companies or groups, the butchers, the shoemakers, the woollen drapers and the mercers. This enabled them to weald much power and influence over the town because no man could carry out business of any kind unless he had first served an apprenticeship and then been admitted as a freeman to one of the companies.

Tradesmen who did not meet these qualifications were known as 'foreigners' and were fined if they were caught attempting to trade illegally. This gave the guilds a monopoly in the town. By 1540 Kingston was described as: "The bestie market towne of all Southerey".

The arrival of the Royal Household just upriver at Hampton Court Palace was huge for Kingston. Firstly, the place had to be built, meaning that great amounts of local timber and locally manufactured bricks were used by local artisans to construct the building. And, once completed, it had to be serviced. Extra food and wine and other supplies were also needed to keep the Royals and their many visitors happy.

Charles I then granted yet another charter to the town stipulating that no other market may be held within a seven-mile radius, effectively blocking competition. Needless to say, this helped the market become even more prosperous.

The town grew to become an important stopover for the ever increasing numbers of coaches passing through on their way south and west. Coaching inns and taverns sprung up all around the market place. The Druid's Head remains today, although the arrival of railways saw the inns begin to close through lack of trade.

The market also slowly diminished in importance as the 20th century progressed. It has recently been revamped, though, and is now thriving once again, still selling fruit and veg, alongside specialist stalls selling food from all over the world. Visit this historic market any day of the week, particularly at lunch time, and you will find a place buzzing with activity. Hopefully, it may last another 800 years!

Below left: Monthly antiques market, the Old London Road   Opposite: Having fun in the Market Square

Cafe society, spoilt for choice

'Flock of mallard ducks', Charter Quay

The Antiques Market

High Street

Home Park fallow deer

Dry grass in the evening sun, Home Park and Bushy Park

Opposite: Around and about Ham Pond

Right: Kingston Crematorium

autumn

Richmond Park

The Thames in autumn

St Raphael's Catholic Church

Hampton Wick Pond, Home Park

Longford River, Bushy Park

Recent Times

Kingston remained pretty much the same throughout the 18th century, pootling along nicely as a successful market and trading town and transport hub for the coaching business. With the coming of the railway and a subsequent population explosion, the town was transformed, however, in the 19th century.

Agriculture became less important once residents could commute to work in London. New stations at Surbiton and New Malden meant that Kingston had its own suburbs. The population grew from 5,000 in 1811 to 34,375 by 1901.

By the end of the Victorian era a new drainage system replaced Kingston's old open ditches full of raw sewage that would run through the town. Now, there was clean, piped drinking water, a workhouse infirmary (that later became Kingston Hospital) to treat the sick and poor, while a slum clearance got rid of inadequate, unhealthy housing. Things were looking up, as Kingston became an even more attractive place to live.

Traffic soon became a problem, with the town's narrow, medieval street layout making transport planning difficult. Kingston bypass, which opened in 1927, was one of the first in the country, designed to ease congestion. But the area was actively promoted as an attractive place to live and work in the 1930s, leading to new factories and housing estates, an even larger population – and more traffic jams.

The London General Omnibus Company opened Kingston bus garage in 1922. By 1964 recruitment issues and cost-cutting led to the introduction of one-man operated buses, which were first trialed in Kingston. And the town claimed another first when Jill Viner became London's first woman bus driver in 1974.

In 1935 a new Guildhall was built, incorporating law courts, municipal offices, council chamber and committee rooms. In 2011, Kingston Magistrates Court, housed in the building, was shut in a government cost-cutting exercise, meaning that, for the first time in 800-years, Kingston didn't have its own local court system. It does, however, boast a Crown Court, situated on the Penrhyn Road, which deals with high-profile criminal cases.

After the devastation of the Second World War there was a necessity to move on and look to the future. Post-war it became fashionable to knock down old buildings and rebuild using new construction materials such as concrete. Kingston did not escape this trend and many historic old buildings were demolished to make way for the 1960s-style architecture.

The town's architecture today, is a reflection of its historical growth: a combination of very old buildings that survived the purge, Victorian housing, pre- and post-war housing estates, 1960s tower blocks and 1980s department stores. In other words, a hotch-potch of styles.

In recent years there has been an effort to emphasise Kingston's identity as a historic market town, revitalising the town centre by pedestrianising the main shopping area and re-developing the riverside. The return of a theatre to the town has boosted its cultural credentials enormously, but that is not without controversy, as the popular Rose Theatre is subsidised by the council.

Overall, though, despite a few hiccups, Kingston is a very attractive and pleasant place to work, visit and live.

The Rose Theatre

'Paper Trail' sculpture on College Roundabout

The Rotunda

View from the Bentall Centre

Education

One of the most desirable reasons to move to the borough of Kingston is the quality of the education it provides, possessing high calibre state and private schools and a highly respected university.

Provision of education in the town goes back hundreds of years. There is evidence of a public school in Kingston dating back to the Middle Ages, and in 1561 Queen Elizabeth I signed a charter establishing the "free grammar school of Queen Elizabeth for the education training and instruction of boys and youths in grammar". In 1904 this school became Kingston Grammar, now considered one of the most successful co-educational schools in England.

Kingston is one of the few boroughs in England that still has grammar schools operating alongside comprehensive schools. Its two grammar schools, Tiffin Boys' and Tiffin Girls', owe their existence to a couple of prosperous brothers, John and Thomas Tiffin, who made their fortune from brewing and left money in their wills in 1638 for the education of local children. At first the money was used for scholarships to attend local schools. However, the fund grew through investment returns and additional donations, so by the 1820s nearly 110 children were benefiting from their legacy. Then, in 1874, plans were drawn up for the establishment of two new schools; Tiffin Boys' School and Tiffin Girls' School. Each admitted 150 pupils, and opened in January 1880.

In 1929, the Boys' School moved to its present site, in Queen Elizabeth Road, near the centre of Kingston. It became a grammar school under the Education Act of 1944. In 1937, a new building on the Richmond Road was opened for the Girls' School. Today both schools are thriving with a thousand pupils in each, and both granted outstanding status by Ofsted.

Further education is also well catered for with a successful college and university located in the town. The origins of both date back to 1899, when the Royal Borough of Kingston-upon-Thames built Science and Art Schools and a Technical Institute on the present main site of the College in Kingston Hall Road. The Victorian home of Kingston Technical College (as the institution was then known) survived until the 1960s, when major reconstruction work followed a local reorganisation of further and higher education. In 1962 Kingston Technical College split into the present college of further education and a college of technology, now Kingston University.

Because Kingston College and Kingston University have this common heritage, there remains a strong bond between them today. Jointly run courses and close staff relations ensure that a ladder of educational opportunity is available for both full-time and part-time students from post-GCSE to first degree levels, and beyond.

In 1992 Kingston became a university town when Kingston Polytechnic, rated the best in the country at the time, was granted University status. The campus is spread all over the town swelling the population by 23,000 in term time.

Left: Kingston Art College
Below: One of the University buses
Opposite: Kingston Grammar School

The band 'To Kill a King' play in one of the regular live music concerts held in All Saints Church

New Malden

New Malden is a relatively recent addition as a suburb of Kingston, but is unique because of its large Korean population. Until 1846 Malden was a small, sleepy village situated by the Hogsmill River, but with the coming of the railways that all changed. A branch line joining Kingston to Wimbledon and a station built on uninhabited farmland just north of the village saw the beginning of the population rise in the area and the creation of New Malden.

The station was originally built to service a few wealthy residents who lived nearby in Coombe, but a local entrepreneur named John King saw the potential for development and bought 93 acres of land around the station. His hunch turned out to be right and he ended up making a fortune with New Malden growing and thriving around the central hub of the station. The population has increased steadily over the last 150 years with an ever growing Korean influx since the 1970s.

So why have Koreans chosen to settle in New Malden in such numbers? Its popularity has been attributed to the former residence of the South Korean ambassador in Lord Chancellor Walk, in nearby Coombe Lane West. In the 1970s compatriots followed the ambassador's lead and settled in the area. The Korean electronic giant Samsung also based its UK headquarters in New Malden until its 2005 move to Chertsey in Surrey. Some cite a joint-venture between Racal Avionics (previous Decca) and a Korean chaebol (business conglomerate) in the 1950s as the start of the community.

Just under 29,000 people live in New Malden; upwards of 10,000 of them are Koreans. The vast majority are from South Korea, although at least 600 political refugees from North Korea also are resident – the largest population anywhere outside Korea. New Malden is popular because here, new arrivals can speak Korean, eat Korean food, frequent Korean businesses and spend time with fellow Koreans.

The High Street is dotted with a wide range of authentic Korean shops, restaurants and businesses with many of the street signs written in Hangeul as well as English. The area is proud to offer a cultural experience unlike anywhere else in the UK, which is celebrated all year round but particularly at the annual Korean Festival.

The annual Malden Fortnight Festival, which hosts a range of fun and cultural events organised by the local community, is another highlight in the social calendar.

Korean culture in Kingston

The market characters and specialty stalls

Home Park

Home Park (also known as Hampton Court Park) is the smallest of the Royal parks that surround the town. It is not that small, however, covering an area of 750 acres from the Hampton Wick side of Kingston Bridge all the way to Hampton Court – a glorious three-mile walk if you follow the river.

It may be the least known and least used of the parks, but Home Park is a tranquil gem with its herd of 300 fallow deer, several pretty ponds and the magnificent Long Water, stretching a mile from the palace, bordered by an avenue of lime trees. Similar avenues of trees radiate out from the palace in all directions, forming long green corridors with vistas of the famous building.

Hampton Wick Pond, just inside the park entrance, is within spitting distance of the town. It is full of wildfowl and surrounded by bullrushes and weeping willows. A peaceful haven next to a busy town. Another pond, known as Rick Pond, is a longer walk from the entrance but on Sundays it is worth a stroll to see the members of Hampton Court Model Yacht Club racing their remote-controlled boats. The club has been in existence since the 1890s and races are held weekly come rain or shine. The pond's water comes from the River Longford, which feeds all the ornamental gardens of Hampton Court, flowing down the Long Water into the Rick Pond before departing into the River Thames. The Longford River isn't actually a river at all, it's a 12 mile man-made canal running from the River Colne in the village of Longford (near Heathrow Airport), all the way to the Thames. It was built for King Charles I in 1638/39 as a water supply for the ornamental Hampton Court Palace fountains as there wasn't enough water pressure from the Thames to drive them.

At the end of the Long Water is the Jubilee Fountain, built as a historic tribute to mark Queen Elizabeth's 50 years on the British throne.

The Jubilee Fountain is a simple but striking design, consisting of five jets of water to mark each decade of The Queen's reign. The largest of the jets, at nearly 100 feet in height, sits between four supporting 30 foot jets as a splendid addition to Hampton Court Palace gardens.

The Long Water Canal was created in 1660 as part of the preparations by King Charles II for the arrival of his bride, Catherine of Braganza. It was meant as a ceremonial canal upon which the new Queen would arrive in a long procession to meet her future husband. The Long Water Canal ends within the East Front Gardens of Hampton Court Palace, an area originally known as the Great Fountain Garden because it contained 13 ornamental fountains.

Every year the Hampton Court Palace Flower Show takes place in the park at the beginning of July. The first show was held in 1990. This was staged jointly by the Historic Royal Palaces and the rail company, Network South East, in an effort to raise revenue for both organisations. Special trains were laid on from Waterloo, and porters wore carnations in their hats to create a buzz around the show. Even though there was comparatively little trade support for the show, it drew in large crowds. The RHS took over running it in 1993 and today it is the largest flower show in the world, spreading over 25 acres of the park straddling the Long Water.

Near the entrance of the park at Kingston is the ice house, a subterranean structure built and used for the storage of ice and, in turn, the preservation of food. When ice is packed together, its relatively small surface area slows down the thawing process. The ice lasted longer if kept at a regular low temperature and insulated by straw, thick walls and a roof.

The ice house is located close to the Thames in order to easily harvest ice in the depths of winter. Ice houses also have a drain hole in the base for the slow-melting ice to drain away. However, because of it's temperature control efficiency, a full ice house could take up to 18 months to thaw. James I of England commissioned the construction of the first modern ice house in Greenwich Park in 1619 and another to be built at Hampton Court in 1625. It is now a Grade II listed building.

The park is also home to a golf club that was established in 1895 two years after Queen Victoria had opened the park for public use. It started life as a 9 hole course known as Home Park Golf Club, but is now called Hampton Court GC, and boasts an 18 hole course. There is an oak tree called 'the medieval oak' situated beside one of the tees that is thought to be 750 years old.

Stud House in the middle of the park was built in the early 18th century to house the Master of the Horse, a post traditionally held by an aristocratic royal favourite. The Royal stud used to be located in the park and many race horses were bred there and grazed in the lush paddocks, a few of which remain in the north west corner of the park.

The house is now owned by the Russian Evgeny Lebedev. He is famous for being the son of Alexander Lebedev a KGB officer turned billionaire businessman. He made a name for himself by buying the Evening Standard and The Independent to become the youngest newspaper proprietor in the UK. For the past few years, Lebedev has been restoring the house to something like its former glory. "I wanted it to be the most beautiful country house in London again," he said.

Swans on the Rick Pond, Home Park

Left: Ham Pond
Right: Ham Common
Bottom right: Ham Lands

The Long Water, Hampton Court Palace in Home Park

The Towpath in autumn

Above: '60s style

Opposite: Inside the Bentall Centre

Fairfield in the autumn

index

Thank you to the staff at Gibson Lane estate agents for their kind support of our book.

Independent estate agents for Kingston upon Thames and Ham

KINGSTON BRANCH

34 Richmond Road
Kingston upon Thames
Surrey KT2 5ED

020 8546 5444

HAM BRANCH

323 Richmond Road
Ham
Surrey KT2 5QU

020 8247 9444

gibsonlane.co.uk

We value your home

All rights reserved. No part of this publication may be reproduced, stored in any retrieval system or transmitted in any form or by any means, electronic, mechanical photocopying or otherwise without the prior permission of the copyright holders. Whilst every care has been taken in the production of this book, no responsibility can be accepted for any errors or omissions. The publishers have taken all reasonable care in compiling this work but cannot accept responsibility for the information derived from third parties, which has been reproduced in good faith.

First Edition – © Unity Print and Publishing Limited 2017

Designed by Ball Design & Branding, www.balldesignconsultancy.com
Printed by Page Brothers of Norwich, Norfolk. www.pagebros.co.uk
Colour Management by Paul Sherfield of The Missing Horse Consultancy. www.missinghorsecons.co.uk
Proof reading: Caroline MacMillan
Published by Andrew Wilson, Unity Print and Publishing Limited, 18 Dungarvan Avenue, London SW15 5QU.
Tel: +44 (0)20 8487 2199 aw@unity-publishing.co.uk www.unity-publishing.co.uk Twitter: @andrewpics